Dear Parents and Educators,

Welcome to Puffin Young Readers! As par( know that each child develops at his or her speech, critical thinking, and, of course, reu....,. recognizes this fact. As a result, each Puffin Young Readers book is assigned a traditional easy-to-read level (1–4) as well as a Guided Reading Level (A–P). Both of these systems will help you choose the right book for your child. Please refer to the back of each book for specific leveling information. Puffin Young Readers features esteemed authors and illustrators, stories about favorite characters, fascinating nonfiction, and more!

## Frances Dances

**LEVEL 2**
**GUIDED READING LEVEL F**

This book is perfect for a **Progressing Reader** who:
- can figure out unknown words by using picture and context clues;
- can recognize beginning, middle, and ending sounds;
- can make and confirm predictions about what will happen in the text; and
- can distinguish between fiction and nonfiction.

Here are some **activities** you can do during and after reading this book:
- Make Connections: In this story, Frances loves to dance. But when she gets scared to dance onstage, she stops dancing completely. Have you ever been too scared to do something? What were you afraid of, and how did you overcome your fear?
- Read the Pictures: Use the pictures in this book to tell the story. Have the child go through the book, retelling the story just by looking at the pictures.

Remember, sharing the love of reading with a child is the best gift you can give!

—Bonnie Bader, EdM
   Puffin Young Readers program

*Puffin Young Readers are leveled by independent reviewers applying the standards developed by Irene Fountas and Gay Su Pinnell in *Matching Books to Readers: Using Leveled Books in Guided Reading*, Heinemann, 1999.

To Ally and Tyler, the best dancers
in the world—MI

PUFFIN YOUNG READERS
Published by the Penguin Group
Penguin Group (USA) LLC, 375 Hudson Street, New York, New York 10014, USA

USA | Canada | UK | Ireland | Australia | New Zealand | India | South Africa | China

penguin.com
A Penguin Random House Company

Penguin supports copyright. Copyright fuels creativity, encourages diverse voices, promotes free speech,
and creates a vibrant culture. Thank you for buying an authorized edition of this book
and for complying with copyright laws by not reproducing, scanning, or distributing any part of it
in any form without permission. You are supporting writers and allowing Penguin to continue
to publish books for every reader.

Copyright © 2015 by Mark Iacolina. All rights reserved. Published by Puffin Young Readers, an imprint
of Penguin Group (USA) LLC, 345 Hudson Street, New York, New York 10014. Manufactured in China.

Library of Congress Cataloging-in-Publication Data is available.

ISBN 978-0-448-48992-6 (pbk)                     10 9 8 7 6 5 4 3 2 1

PUFFIN YOUNG READERS

LEVEL 2
PROGRESSING READER

# Frances Dances

by Mark Iacolina

Puffin Young Readers
An Imprint of Penguin Group (USA) LLC

This is Frances.

Every morning, Frances dances.

Frances dances out of bed.

Frances dances down the stairs.

Frances dances at the table.

Frances dances and dances!

But she does not dance

out the door.

And she never dances at school.

Today, Frances's teacher has a surprise.

The class is going to dance.

They are going to dance on a real stage!

But Frances does not want

to dance with her class.

And she does not want

to dance on a real stage.

All day, her class dances and dances.

But not Frances.

That night, Frances tells her mom she will not dance onstage. Her mom tells Frances that everyone loves to watch her dance.

But Frances is not so sure.

The next morning, Frances does not dance.

She does not dance out of bed.

She does not dance

down the stairs.

She does not dance at the table.

But her mom dances.

And her dad dances.

Even her brother dances.

Everyone dances.

But not Frances.

Every day, the class dances.

But not Frances.

Finally, it is the day of the show.

Frances is on the stage

with her class.

She closes her eyes.

She sees her mom dancing.

She sees her dad dancing.

She sees her brother dancing.

The music starts.

Frances opens her eyes.

She has a ribbon.

She has wings.

She has a tutu!

Her foot begins to tap.

Frances smiles.

She is not scared.

Frances dances!